What a Re-imagined Society Looks Like

(and how we can get there from here.)

A PRACTICAL

GUIDEBOOK

FROM FUTURIST

CHET W. SISK

Contents

Introduction

In November of 2020, Federal Reserve Chairman Jerome Powell stated: "the economy (in the US) that we knew, might be over." That means it's time to create something new. He's indicating that the COVID pandemic has rewritten the rules of how everything works.

In the spirit of his statement, I want to ask you to indulge me for a moment and use your visionary skills. Visualize a different kind of economy and society than the one we have. One that is stronger, more abundant, empowering, and sharing. This is what I see . . .

In many of our communities, we would have a multicultural, cross-gender board of elders—people 70 years or older who are trained negotiators and mediators. They provide advice to the governing body on issues relating to the direction of the community. This board also provides rulings on personal and major disputes from a restorative justice lens. While they cannot override decisions by elected officials, their verdict on issues is a major factor when the governing body makes decisions.

In those same communities, teams of entrepreneurs and freelancers are building projects and businesses that increase the quality of life for every one and help our resiliency in the face of crises of scale—from climate change to regular and consistent pandemics. From food security options to the deployment of electric cars as public utility to organized ways of using a cleaner, environmentally "green cement" for new sustainable building homes.

This same community has established a private equity fund that seeks to provide seed and start-up resources to enterprises that serve the greater good of the community. Everything from food security operations to childcare gets priority in this fund.

A priority of this community is to host regular and consistent block parties that provide tax incentives or other benefits for people to leave the comfort of the communities they know to spend time in the communities of people they don't know.

The beat walking police teams are now made up of a peace officer and a mental health professional who help diagnose crises and seek ways to diffuse a situation. More of the city resources are directed toward empowering communities instead of isolating them.

Food is no longer chemically treated and void of its initial nutrients. It no longer has to be labeled between organic and non-organic because it *all* is organic. We incorporate a well-organized system of backyard gardening with hydroponics and local distribution, making sure it is accessible in all parts of the community.

A new kind of city-wide infrastructure is created around the philosophical construct of "Ubuntu" -- everything and everyone is connected. All decisions from the governing body start from the fundamental question of how those decisions affect the quality of life of everyone and everything in the community.

The push for growth is replaced with the push for quality of life where everyone can live lives of dignity and abundance.

These communities are connected, sharing resources and information with each other in a transparent, accessible, and easy-to-read website. Civics classes are now mandatory for all students. Voting is mandatory for all citizens. The 1619 project is part of all school curricula. This community bands with other communities to disband the for-profit criminal justice system and eliminate their position in 401K portfolios.

Along with Ubuntu as a guiding principle, Feminine Principle Leadership becomes the leadership model of the day, with leaders now creating policies that starts with the question "Is everyone going to be alright with this proposal?"

It's not that some of these approaches are not being leveraged in a lot of our communities, but in the world I created, these would be our priorities.

To some of you, this scenario seems hopelessly unrealistic. But then, you have to first ask the question, why do you believe that? As a former advertising entrepreneur, I have discovered is that what we might think of as "not realistic" is more a result of you being "trained" or what used to be called "brainwashed" to *believe* it is unrealistic. I wrote a book a few years ago called *Think This - Not That* to more closely examine the idea of "conventional wisdom." What I discovered was that what some people say is unrealistic is really an idea handed down to them, without data, facts, details, proof, or due diligence. Many of you would be stunned by the amount of false data we hold up as guiding principles in our lives.

The challenges of the moment are asking us to question those false assumptions and ask the most basic question of all: "Can't we do better than this?" The answer is, of course, we can, but the entrenchment of false and destructive thought is strong.

Along with my travels around the world teaching transition management as a Futurist, I taught a personal development class at a homeless shelter for 12 years in Denver, Colorado. The most important thing I learned from that experience is that fear is a strong motivator. The only emotion I know that's strong enough to challenge the supremacy of fear is hope. From my experiments at the shelter, I realized that if people have a vision for something greater than what they are experiencing, a hope, then they can walk through fire to get to that. That is what this book is all about. First the vision, at least my version of what that vision could be. Then the road map necessary for us to walk through the fear of the moment.

I want to be clear, this is not a treatise on any particular economic system born in the 20th century, so please, stop with the labeling. It's only a hard look at what's not working and how we can stop doing the same thing over and over again and expect different results.

Check out how we can get there . . .

1

How the Western diet is making us sicker, poorer, and dumber.

Often times when people think about ways of impacting the world to transform it, they miss the most obvious and direct ways of doing it. They are in search of the grand, the spectacular, and the most demonstrable. There is one thing we can all do that is much more low-key but carries the biggest punch. Quit eating the Western diet.

The Western diet or the Standard American diet is a modern dietary pattern that is generally characterized by high intakes of red meat, processed meat, prepackaged foods, butter, candy and sweets, fried foods, conventionally raised animal products, high-fat dairy products, eggs, refined grains, potatoes, corn and high-fructose corn syrup, and high sugar. This poisonous flow of manufactured food-like substances invented and globally distributed by the West is one of the most dangerous things ever invented in the history of humankind. Need proof?

The Western diet is linked to diminishing brain function.

Several studies have come out over the past few years that point to something that seems obvious . . . if you eat enough fries, hamburgers, sugary, fatty, processed, and salt-laden food, you get dumber. Researchers in the Psychology Department at Macquire University in Sydney, Australia, enlisted 110 healthy participants aged between 20 and 23 in their investigation, splitting them into a control group who ate a good diet, and another who consumed a high-energy Western diet including a hearty portion of Belgian waffles and fast food. Their findings? Continued exposure to the Western diet directly affects parts of the brain that deal with memory and the ability to draw on data to make informed choices. These initial subtle impairments may lead to dementia and declines in brain performance, Professor Stevenson said.

If you have kids who are on the Western diet, their future is being sabotaged. If you have parents and they are eating this stuff, they are greatly increasing the odds of dementia and Alzheimer's disease. If you don't seem to be as sharp as you thought you were at one time, it may have everything to do with that steady diet of fast food you've made part of your daily routine.

The Western diet is diminishing your ability to fight COVID-19.

The more of the Western diet you take into your system, the less you get of the proper nutrients and vitamins necessary for your health defense. Optimal health is always your best defense against an invasive virus. In a September 17, 2020, edition of *The Conversation*, an investigative study revealed that along with social distancing measures and effective vaccines, a healthy immune system is our best defense against Corona virus infection. To keep it that way, proper nutrition is an absolute must. Although not a replacement for medicine, good nutrition can work with medicine to improve vaccine effectiveness, reduce the prevalence of chronic disease, and lower the burden on the health care system.

The Western diet is literally killing you.

Hope you're enjoying that hamburger! If you have regular intakes of Western Diet food, you've probably shaved 20 years off your life span. You've also greatly contributed to the diminishing of your quality of life through the heart disease and hypertension. In a Sentient Media article of January 2019, the finger of diminished quality of life and increased deaths all pointed to the Western diet. The authors say when the food we eat doesn't provide the nutrients that we need, it's hard for us to feel "full." When we don't feel full, we keep eating.

This is a dangerous cycle as people continuously eat low-quality, highly processed foods that play a major role in the deterioration of people's health.

The Western diet is adding to our climate change disaster.

In order to meet the demands of the fast-food industry, more and more of our natural forests will have to be dedicated to raising cattle and pigs. Not only does that diminish the earth's natural tools in balancing CO_2 emissions, but the methane produced by the massive industrial farms increases CO_2 output. When climate-change people talk about *reducing* your intake of meat, they're not trying to "take away your burgers." They just ran the numbers and realized that there is a low-risk, highly participatory action all of us can do right now to save our future. In a recent study in the journal *Nature*, doing more to expand Western-style diets on more tables will drive an escalation of forests cleared for increased meat production. Feeding the growing guest list will also increase fuel expenditures to operate tractors, seagoing trawlers, refrigerators, fertilizer production, transportation, and industrial food processing plants.

The Western diet is the force behind the world obesity epidemic.

Wherever Western civilization spreads in the world, the Western diet goes with it and so does the global obesity epidemic. Societies that had a relatively strong health index among its people prior to the invasion of fast-food chains and sugary items from the US are now battling with obesity at a phenomenal rate.

The Western diet is incredibly addictive.

There's a reason you're finding it difficult to quit eating something that directly diminishes your quality of life as well as destroys the planet. Simply put, the amount of processed sugar has the ability to block the brain's ability to determine that it is full. Thus, it makes you feel like you need more. It is in the same league as any other controlled substance.

What can I do?

There have been healthy, more humane diets that have existed eons before the rise of the Western diet. They include a vegan diet, a vegetarian diet, the Mediterranean diet, the West African diet, and any plant-based diet that better mimics what our ancestors *actually* ate. And no, it's not keto.

Put the oxygen mask on yourself first before you seek to save the other passengers on the plane. Get rid of the Western diet.

2

We need new "conventional wisdom."

There are a lot of destructive ideas that have been floating around society, masquerading as "conventional wisdom," or shared wisdom in the best interest of society. Now is the time to introduce some essential wisdom to a world that demands it.

Let's break the belief that shareholder value is everything.

Moving global corporations away from their singular fixation on maximizing shareholder value and getting them to focus on the quality of life in communities will be a step in the right direction in salvaging life on earth. When shareholder value is your obsession, it means anyone and anything can be exploited by the company to produce profit—even at the expense of our survival as a species. In the United States, the Business Roundtable, a non-profit association based in Washington, D.C., whose members are chief executive officers of major companies, pronounced in 2019 that they were moving away from the shareholder-value-is-everything model and moving to a more holistic approach to corporation/consumer relationship. So far - crickets.

Let's forward progressive tax codes.

I'll use another example from the United States. From 1945 to 1975, the US saw a level of growth unparalleled in modern history. During the presidential administrations of Franklin Roosevelt, Truman, Eisenhower, Kennedy, Johnson, Nixon, Ford, and Carter, the top-tax-bracket rate was at least 70 percent, and for long periods was much more. (John Kennedy's tax-cut plan of the early 1960s took the top rate from 90 percent down to 70 percent.) This money went directly to empowering communities and taking care of the common good. The Nordic States of Denmark, Norway, The Netherlands, and Finland have championed a higher tax rate and regularly rate in the top 10 as the best quality of life countries in the world. Of course, the application can vary around the world, but making taxes more progressive to take care of the greater good is a powerful first step.

Let's re-evaluate the gospel of growth.

Change and transformation management means everything is put on the table for a good look over. We now need to have a grown-up conversation about unlimited growth. Is it good? Is it bad? In a finite world, does it even make sense? Are there other ways of doing growth during change and transition? Director of Strategy for a global collective called The Rules, Martin Kirk asked two basic questions in a 2019 article: "What if growth isn't as positive as you think? If we don't quickly create a new economy that isn't based on constant expansion, we will run out of Earth." Having the conversation isn't a sin. Not having it is.

Let's take a close look at Universal Basic Income ... again.

A twelve-year Universal Basic Income (UBI) study provided by the GiveDirectly charity in Kenya arrived at three distinct results.

A. People tend to spend free cash on necessities.

B. Contrary to prevailing myths, people in the UBI program don't work less or waste money on vices like alcohol.

C. The community where the UBI families lived actually became richer because the families spent their money in their communities.

The idea of giving money without strings to families has been around for years, but the ongoing income inequality gap has helped the idea of giving people a basic income (no questions asked) and has gained the attention of communities around the world. Other studies are still in the works, but the preliminary data says people don't become lazy after receiving free money; they actually become more industrious.

Let's tie challenge and opportunity together.

In case it hasn't hit home yet, we are living in very interesting times. As interesting times go, both wolves live among us—the one that will drag us to hell and the other one that will lead us to a greater world. Which wolf we feed is being decided at this time. As a trend analyst, I am observing, in real time, what decisions we're making and how they will impact the immediate future. I advocate for the feeding of the opportunity wolf, but our views of what an opportunity is and what a challenge is differ widely. It becomes crucial that we understand that our mind is very adept at playing tricks on us, sometimes making everything a point of danger. There are large swaths of citizens in societies around the world right now that are actively engaged in profound disassociation with the facts in an effort to hold onto a certain set of values. You may be one of them. All of us are vulnerable.

The key to future decision-making is not disassociation or pretending that the challenges do not exist. But rather, creating room for both challenge and opportunity in thinking through the challenge, then creating an answer that accounts for both. Creating an either/or zero-sum thinking process is an old world dichotomy that sees the world in stark, unrealistic terms. It's not this or that. It's this and that, and that, and that.

The term "crisis" is saddled with negativity. However, one of the formal definitions of crisis is the turning point of a disease when an important change takes place, indicating either recovery or death.

Let's step up the test driving of alternative economies.

The new world emerging is coming at a heavy cost. The economic challenges which the world has not experienced since the Great Depression are now here. The COVID-19 pandemic has exposed that old economic models are not sustainable. It has also helped us understand how vulnerable we all are to problems that may seem regional or local. This vulnerability has left the door open to leveraging the global ties, but through more robust and agile models that work better. In other words, there are other economic models that are better at handling the challenges of the future than the models we may be currently using. Here are some that we may want to consider for our communities.

The Sharing Economy: This model, based on the idea of sharing technology, spaces, and opportunities, is simply suggesting that the sharing of resources is much more economically efficient and effective than what we have been using for the past few centuries. It uses trust as a primary currency and has developed fail-safes for trust defaults.

The Gift Economy: This newly emerging idea is social media–based and designed to have all production donate a portion of the gross to life-sustaining institutions and problems. It "gifts" a portion of everything we make, produce, or distribute to greater social causes, like universal health care, eliminating hunger, and ending poverty.

The Collaborative Commons/Zero Marginal Cost Economy: This new economic system positions itself as the successor to capitalism in that it takes advantage of technologies of efficiency and serves the public good much better than anything we have created before. The premise is simple: we now have the technology to make basic goods and services (food, utilities, information goods, etc.) free. This stabilizes the markets and allows us to direct new resources into innovative ideas to empower society and the planet.

The Ubuntu Economy: This idea is based on the South African philosophical concept that we are all connected to each other as humans and to the greater world of animals, the environment, and all living things. This economy is not necessarily based on hard infrastructure as much as it is based on the idea that all things are connected. Once that is established, the economic direction is to now create systems that understand everything is dependent on other things. This changes separation, individualism, and self-serving vehicles and discourages unilateral action. It encourages collaborative, work-together models.

The Circular Economy: This economic model challenges the very foundation of the fossil energy–economic model. In this model, the manufacturers maintain ownership of the products they produce, instead of people purchasing the product individually. The manufacturer is now responsible for the maintenance, upkeep, updating, and fixing of the products. Instead of the product going to the dump after we are done using it, the product goes back to the manufacturer, and the consumer is provided with a new one. The resources the old item has are now back with the manufacturer. The consumer provides a monthly or yearly fee to the manufacturer for the service, and that fee costs less than the purchase.

These are only some of the new economic models. The bottom line is that there are tons of new economic models that we now have the opportunity to pursue in this new world emerging that is asking us to expand our possibilities.

Let's get communities to host vision parties.

The great challenge that seems to show up regularly in our current leadership and social circles is that vision is seen as a kind of exotic fruit. It is "nice-to-have" occasionally for variety and to feel good, but it's never really seen as a standard tool for everyday success. Even more, the current vision of many of our leaders is on lack, fear, and scarcity. Thus, with their resources, they create political, religious, economic, and social structures that reflect their vision. This is why vision parties are critical. You must develop vision parties where you and trusted friends get together over pizza, snacks, coffee, tea and talk out loud about your biggest, most empowering dreams and visions not just for you, but for your communities. Developing a vision helps people understand what may lie beyond the immediate horizon and help communicate what those possibilities and challenges may be. Merely following the status quo may even be a sign that a society has died and run out of fresh ideas to reinvent itself. Vision creates a formal infrastructure for thinking ahead. Vision development is not an exotic fruit. In a time of change, it is the lifeline between what was and what could and will be.

Let's embrace test practices instead of best practices.

We are going to step away from the term "best practices" for now and lean into another one that may be appropriate for the times. Let us list a series of "test practices" that we should be putting into action now. Some of them are tests because they have not been implemented before. The same could be said for what we now call "best practices." Someone had to test them out at some point to find which ones worked.

Let's incorporate the faith community into messaging.

Belief is the central part of this plan. If there is not a shared belief in the idea of an empowered and abundant future, it will be hard for people to embrace it. A shared belief is not one that everyone agrees to. Rather, it is one that all faiths socialize in their temples, their churches, their synagogues, and other places of worship. Having your local leaders of faith share a simple message like "new possibilities are being born every day" or "we're better together" or "let's envision a new world" is consistent with the basic tenants of their faith. Joint messaging in sermons, bumper stickers, banners, and websites goes a long way to bring clarity to the new normal. Remember the basics of understanding media: repeated messages affect behavior.

Let's bring back victory gardens.

During World War II, many British and American households engaged in creating victory gardens as a way to produce surplus food supplies for communities and cities. This should be a community campaign that helps support the food infrastructure during the crisis and minimizes food insecurity challenges throughout many parts of the world. Even more, it provides a kind of "esprit de corps" (rallying of the troops) among the general public so that we all know we're in this forward-thinking process together. Hunger has been an issue in our world for decades but was exposed and expanded even more by COVID-19 through the massive job losses.

These approaches help create the infrastructure of a new normal. It is not beyond our ability to create a community that works better and more efficiently than what we've embraced in the past. The key is to get these approaches in place so that the community is robust enough to endure the challenges, black swans, missteps, and another pandemic. But once they are in place, they give you a foundation on which to build on.

An infrastructure built on these ideas will help make the new normal a time for retooling, regeneration, and re-imagination.

3

Stop pretending that homelessness of scale is an inevitable part of progress. It's not.

Did you know that there are over 30 empty homes per person in the United States? Seems almost incredible that we have a homelessness crisis. But to be fair, the homelessness crisis is caused by a variety of truths in this society, including mental health and drug abuse issues, underpaying jobs that keep the working class unable to save for a home, and, as we found out during the 2008 Great Recession, racially unjust and predatory housing profiteers. Here are a few other caveats that maintain the imbalance between the homeless and houses:

- Some homes stand empty because they are some people's second home.

- Some are empty because they are so far off the beaten path, few people want to live in those remote places.

- Some of the houses are only temporarily empty as they are in the midst of being vacant between occupants.

- Some of those homes are simply abandoned. They are dilapidated and have yet to be refurbished or torn down.

Some would point to all of these points and say, "See, that's why we have this abundance of homes and homelessness." They would clutch their pearls, wag their fingers, and go about their business as if there was nothing that could be done. That of course is why there is a housing crisis in the first place. There is a lack of will to think more creatively about how we can solve it.

But what if we took a full creative approach and pursued the following ideas? Here are some of that thinking.

Direct our national attention to rural communities.

What if we organized national resources and the newest technology to bring high-speed internet service to more and more rural towns, then provided incentives for people at companies to work remotely from empty rural homes? The whole idea that people should work from concentrated locations in major cities and hubs has been dismantled by the COVID-19 pandemic. People can work from anywhere, as long as there is a decent internet connection. I would even submit, they could work better in smaller towns because their quality of life would be better. This immediately changes the urban housing market by having fewer and fewer young professionals coming into a city and being the tip of the sword of a gentrifying effort by developers.

Organize rural housing to accommodate climate change migrants.

This is an extension of the point I just made. There will be hundreds of thousands, if not millions, of people migrating from the coasts due to the ravages of climate change. This includes the well-to-do who have the resources to leave, as well as the working class and poor who have no choice but to leave. Their first choice is to head to major population hubs in search of a new home and resources, putting even more pressure on tenuous housing situations. Making housing in rural communities available with expanded internet services could be exactly what many people need. Even more, jobs and an expanding tax base can come with these migrating populations.

Rural communities should campaign to get more people due to the population bust and a diminishing tax base.

Did you know that we are at the beginning of a population bust in the US? America has a gigantic infertility crisis that has been made worse by the pandemic. Many young people in the family-creation age group have been working poor jobs with little room to progress. Many of those jobs disappeared with the pandemic, which means even fewer people will have children if they don't have the resources to raise a family. That was already a crisis because of climate change, where many young people decided to go on a climate strike, deciding not to bring young people into a world that is in peril.

Rural communities, again, can help to create low-cost housing and jobs so that those who lost work in the major cities can find similar work in smaller towns. No, these jobs won't pay the same as the city, but the quality of life could be better, and expenses could be a lot lower.

The campaign for multi-generational living.

One of the strangest ideas that emerged from the West in the 40s and 50s was the idea of the nuclear family. A husband, a wife, 2.5 kids, and let's not forget the dog named Fido. This unrealistic look at how families should be organized goes against hundreds of thousands of years of how families actually lived. Extended and extensive families were simply the rule of the day. Nuclear family structures take up more homes and space than necessary. It's time to bring Dad and Mom back home, if they so choose.

Get rid of antiquated and racist zoning laws.

Often times, housing comes down to filing bedrooms. People are looking for safe and regular places to lay their heads so that they can earn a living. But zoning laws make it difficult for people with those extra bedrooms to offer them to those who are looking for them. Often times some of those zoning laws were used as part of racist and discredited zoning laws.

Universal Health Care! In my time as a counselor at a homeless shelter, I noticed that one of the biggest categories of people who became homeless were those who had a significant health challenge in their family. To manage this challenge, the family would exhaust all of their resources, including selling their home (if they had one) and savings to save this loved one. That great sacrifice shouldn't put people on the streets.

In the US, the lack of universal health care is especially difficult for families who are living paycheck to paycheck. That happens to be four of every five US workers. This reality is also true among many who make up to $150,000 per year. With these margins, many citizens are a health crisis away from being homeless. I often talk to groups about how no one issue is separate from other issues. There cannot be "silos" of issues. Providing Universal Health Care can take a giant dent out of homelessness. It can help families keep their hard-earned dollars, thus increasing community wealth, and can help with prevailing health issues that are hampering the quality of life for the vast majority of citizens.

But many of you have heard all of this before. The challenge we face is not the numbers or the logic in making an investment that could stop the falling life expectancy rate in this country. It really comes down to the fact that there are a group of people in the country who don't want some people to have health care because it violates their idea that some people simply aren't deserving of health care, not because of what they do, *but who they are.* With this centuries-old belief firmly in place, another way will have to emerge. One idea is to expand the reach of the new health care cooperatives that are leveraging the new technologies. These start-up companies are cutting the cost of scale through a merging of tele-medicine, health monitor wearables, artificial intelligent diagnoses, a significant dose of preventative health services, 3-D printed devices, and virtual reality treatment. These next-gen health cooperatives are able to cut costs down to an affordable rate for more people and rely more on a patient-nteractive approach with the technology. We're not slaves of the old medical system, but many of us still act as if there is a chain around our ankle. These new emerging cooperatives will at least give us a chance to see that there is an alternative to what we've been told.

It is an international disgrace that any country would have a growing homeless population in a day and age of modern technology, unbridled wealth, and real-world resources. The pressures of our anxiety-driven way of life are behind a lot of this, but there are some infrastructure fixes we could bring to the table right now while we seek to sort out our moral obligation to our neighbors.

4

I bet we can come up with a better way of measuring the well being of a society than the measurement tools we use now.

In the US, there is a full-throated effort at work to redefine wealth and happiness by untying that measurement to the Gross Domestic Product (GDP) and the stock market. During the COVID-19 pandemic, companies made billions of dollars on the stock market. All the while millions of people were losing their jobs and hundreds of thousands were dying because of the virus. There are two realities at work.

Are the GDP and the stock market true measures of our quality of life and happiness?

According to the OECD Better Life Initiative global survey in 2015, most people's answers differed greatly from these two tools. These are the top five wealth measurements by most people according to this survey:

1. Safety

2. Housing

3. Job

4. Income

5. Work–Life Balance

The Pew Research Center did a 2018 survey of Americans and found these five items at the top of the list when it comes to personal wealth:

1. Family

2. Career

3. Money

4. Spirituality and Faith

5. Friends

Richard Barret, a researcher at the Barret Values Center, did a survey of up to a half-million people worldwide to find out what they valued the most. Here are his top five:

1. Family

2. Humor

3. Caring

4. Respect

5. Friendship

It's strange that no one mentions a strong GDP or a rising stock market. In full transparency, this sort of begs the question considering, at least in the US, only half of Americans actually own stock. Yet material gain by any means necessary is the de facto gospel evangelized throughout the West and now spread as the path to success for the rest of the world. Need proof? Look at how we've raised the value of rich people to celebrity and believe they are wiser and better looking than the rest of us. Look at the way we've constantly allowed rich companies to get away with things we would never allow with people or companies of lesser means. Look at how we've allowed our politicians to sell their integrity to the highest bidder, and often for cheap. Look at how we've, collectively, sacrificed the value of other people, creatures, and the planet for the sake of making more money. We are now in the midst of living the consequences of this focus.

Let's not be naive. If I was struggling with two, maybe three jobs to make ends meet and someone shows me a picture of someone living well with a Maserati and a mansion, I too could succumb to the idea that if I can just live that life, my troubles would be over. It's a seductive bait and switch. Work harder and you too can get there. But the reality is that many of the rich and famous didn't get their wealth and fame through hard work, but by legacy gifts, inheritance, well-connected opportunities, and being popular through social media. In my socioeconomic pain, I fall for the okey doke with visions of being one of them.

All of that being said, there is an old saying, "he who dies with the most toys, wins," that's rampant in societies around the world. Entire socioeconomic systems have been created around this core belief. Again, this is inconsistent with what the average person is looking for in a life of dignity, but it is constantly being shoved down our throat through popular culture, advertisement, and our political structures. Perhaps, we can find new ways to measure the well-being of a country that would reflect the values shared in the surveys. Writer Nikita Andester found seven new ways we can determine the health of a country. Allow me to share what she found and wrote about in her research "GDP Alternatives: Seven New Ways of Measuring a Country's Wealth" In Ethical.net·

In 1972, King Jigme Singye Wangchuck of the Buddhist kingdom of Bhutan publicly declared he would no longer seek to grow GDP. Instead, he said, his country would pour its energy into growing their Gross National Happiness (GNH).

What is it?

Guided by Buddhism and mindfulness principles, the king decided that a more spiritual and holistic approach reflected his country's needs. Instead of only looking at the money put towards products and services, GNH takes 9 variables into account:

- living standards

- health

- good governance

- ecological diversity

- resilience

- time use

- psychological wellbeing

- cultural diversity and resilience

- community vitality

To measure these factors, government officials interview a random selection of 8,000 households, who are compensated a day's wage for answering an in-depth questionnaire.

Pros

GNH is one of the most notable alternatives to GDP because it was the first that to be broadly publicised.

It's also remarkably thorough – containing 148 questions (with lengthy sub-questions), the survey examines how residents are doing on every level – from the number of televisions in a home to whether wild animals have impacted their lives.

Cons

The thoroughness of the survey is also a drawback – **answering these questions takes about three hours**, and Bhutan has to pay both the workers interviewing residents and the residents themselves for their time.

Moreover, some people may feel that Bhutan's GNH is too focused on spirituality: some questions in the interview include "Do you meditate?" or "How frequently do you pray?"

And since Bhutan so far is the only country to have developed such a process for interviewing residents, there are currently no curated systems in place for assessing other countries. Unlike GDP, you can't just plug some data points into an equation and get a country's GNH results.

GDP alternatives: Thriving Places Index

What is it?

UK charity **Happy City** developed the Thriving Places Index (TPI) to give local organisers and politicians a better view of the welfare of their people. Since its first run in 2016 assessing 9 cities, it's grown significantly – as of 2019, TPI generated scores for **351 English and 22 Welsh councils**.

TPI's primary focuses are **sustainability, equality, and local conditions**. These three categories are then broken down into 60 indicators. Emphasising local welfare, TPI doesn't do country-wide rankings – instead, it seeks to answer 3 questions about a given area:

1. Is it a fair and equal place to live?

2. Is it sustainable enough so that future generations can flourish?

3. Are the conditions present for everyone to do well?

Happy City has a second project, called the **Happiness Pulse,** which is a micro index for communities, teams, and organisations – kind of like TPI for your workplace.

Pros

By having a local focus, TPI hopes to show exactly **how changing economies impact local communities** – and help governments make more informed decisions about how to care for them.

And unlike GNH, this index could easily be expanded to other parts of the world. Another positive similarity to GNH is the blend of subjective and objective data gathered; the TPI **humanises the subjects of the research, as well as providing hard data on their well being**.

Cons

The blend of objective and subjective data could have its drawbacks. In convincing countries to let go of GDP (a totally numbers-driven index), there could be resistance to the inclusion of subjective input.

GDP alternatives: Happy Planet Index

Photo by Porapak Apichodilok

What is it?

Founded by the **New Economics Foundation,** the Happy Planet Index seeks to measure well being in a new way. By factoring in the **ecological footprint, inequality, well being, and life expectancy of a country**, the HPI provides a simple but rounded glance at the wealth of a country.

They compile their information from a Gallup World Poll, the U.N.'s data on life expectancy, and the Global Footprint Network. And unlike GDP, this index measures equality by investigating how evenly distributed life expectancy and well being are across a country.

To get each country's score, they use this equation:

(life expectancy x experienced well being) x inequality of outcomes

Pros

By pulling data from across different sources, the Happy Planet Index is **easily measurable, flexible, and applicable** to many countries. In addition, dividing people's health and happiness by the size of the carbon footprint puts a country's environmental impact into perspective and dramatically shifts the ranking results.

Cons

The Happy Planet Index has a limited scope. By **only assessing 4 factors**, the data misses some of the nuance of GNH from Bhutan or the Thriving Places Index explore.

How do countries stack up?

- **1st place: Costa Rica**

- **34th: U.K.**

- **72nd: China**

- **108th: U.S.**

- **Last place: Chad**

GDP alternatives: Human Development Index

What is it?

A United Nations Development Programme, the Human Development Index (HDI) was made with a focus on opportunity and capability, rather than just economic growth or environmental sustainability. Interestingly, the U.N. **encourages nations to use it alongside their gross national income data.** They say that it can help governments assess national policy by "asking how two countries with the same level of GNI per capita can end up with different human development outcomes."

Pros

Looking at both education and income per capita is a powerful combination, to see if money and opportunities are actually being funneled to the people. HDI also has the influence of the U.N. on its side, which helps more countries access the data and decide to incorporate it into their decisions.

They also compare the expected years of schooling and the actual mean years of schooling, so that nations can see where communities fall short of expectations – and brainstorm what can be done about it. Combined with life expectancy, these factors give HDI the potential to showcase what opportunity (or lack thereof) looks like in each country.

Cons

While HDI factors in some fundamental metrics, it's **missing a few key ones** like environmental damage, inequality, safety, and empowerment, to name a few – essential aspects of human wellbeing.

How do countries stack up?

- **First place: Norway**

- **13th: U.S.**

- **14th: U.K.**

- **86th: China**

- **Last place: Niger**

GDP alternatives: Green Gross Domestic Product

Photo by Elena Zhuravleva

A spin on traditional GDP, the Green GDP adjusts the measurements by **monetising environmental damage factors** to help countries better understand exactly where they stand environmentally. It was developed by the Chinese government in an attempt to understand the consequences of their carbon emissions and account for the losses they experience from climate change.

Pros

The Green GDP is a noble effort to factor in the cost of climate change in a way that people whose focus is money can appreciate. While subjective data can immediately turn some financially conservative parties off, putting a number on the impact of environmental negligence could potentially hit home.

Cons

The biggest criticism of a Green GDP is that **putting a price on things like loss of biodiversity is difficult and its accuracy debatable**. Environmental impacts like CO_2 emissions are easier to measure – and easier to assign a price to.

And as of now, news on the Green GDP is minimal, making it hard to assess and leaving this experiment to China for the time being.

GDP alternatives: Genuine Progress Indicator

What is it?

Created in the U.S. as an alternative to GDP, the **Genuine Progress Indicator** (GPI) takes into consideration all the same factors as the GDP, while also **accounting for things like the cost of crime, ozone depletion, and lost leisure time**, to paint a more rounded picture of the success of a country.

Pros

One of the main criticisms of GDP is how environmental destruction and natural disasters can boost it. Similarly, GDP is positively affected by perpetuating systems of mass incarceration.

By factoring in environmental, social, and economic indicators together, GPI can give a more rounded assessment of a country's welfare.

Cons

Like many of these other indexes, **GPI hasn't been calculated internationally** – it's only been adopted by a handful of U.S. states. This is one where we'll have to wait to see how it pans out.

GDP alternatives: Better Life Index

The Better Life Index was developed by the Organization for Economic Cooperation and Development (OECD), a group founded in 1961 with one goal: to help governments design better policies to improve lives.

They've identified 11 facets that they feel are essential to wellbeing – **housing, income, jobs, community, education, environment, civic engagement, health, life satisfaction, safety, and work-life balance** – to create the Better Life Index.

First launched in June 2014, the Better Life Index (also known as Regional Well Being) has been gathering data since its inception and has plans to compare current conditions to conditions over time once enough data has been gathered.

Pros

One thing that sets the Better Life Index apart is its **lack of cut-and-dry assessment or ranking**. Instead, the site lets users navigate based on which factors they value most, giving space to create their own opinions based on the data for each facet. It's a cool way to see which regions around the world align with your own values without a value system pre-imposed.

Check out this chart here, where you can click on the measurement you care about the most, and watch the countries rearrange accordingly.

Cons

On the other side of that same coin, when a measurement can't be broken down into easily digestible raw data, it often fails to gain traction.

Aside from that, the Better Life Index is a thoughtful, comprehensive, and promising alternative to GDP.

How do countries stack up?

Although there's no overall ranking, when **sorted according to residents' overall satisfaction**, countries measure up this way:

- **1st place: Norway, Finland, Denmark**

- **15th: U.S.**

- **18th: U.K.**

- **Last place: South Africa**

- **China: no data**

What can we do in the meantime?

These are all thought-provoking alternative ways that *countries* can measure the wealth and well being of their citizens – but what's an individual to do?

The simplest thing you can do is educate others. Tell people there are other ways to measure a country's wealth. If you're a writer, do what I did – write about it. Most importantly, when someone talks about GDP, especially if it's to boast about their own country (fellow U.S. readers, I'm looking at you!), fill them in on its flaws – and suggest an alternative way to measure success.

The key to building a new society is to dump concepts developed during the Industrial Revolution to measure a society in the 21st century. New measurement tools can make sure everyone has the opportunity to live a quality life so that they can leverage the best of their creativity to benefit all of us. That can't happen if people can't feed their families at night. Systemic racism, gender bias, and income inequality are the not-so-invisible hand that leads to greed, lack, graft, malfeasance, and want. This is an opportunity for us to learn from the things that have proven themselves to be failures, and also for us to use our innovative and higher selves to create something greater, better, and more abundant.

5

Building an adaptive society
through adaptive people.

This society tends to talk of being adaptive in a lofty, distant manner, as if being adaptive is a theoretical postulate to be dissected. We hear motivational speakers talk about it in an aspirational way as if it's some goal to be achieved. It's neither one of those versions.

Adaptation is about how our grandparents made a way out of no way. It's about how we scraped by with chewing gum, a rubber band, and paper clips and *somehow* held everything together. This ground level, real-world adaptive lifestyle has to now move from the kitchen table to the board room table. We must now value and promote the kind of thinking that made communities and households resilient.

For the record, scientist Charles Darwin *never* said this: *"It is not the strongest of the species that survives, nor the most intelligent that survives. It is the one that is most adaptable to change."*

However, Darwin's colleagues and disciples forwarded this quote as they read over his notes and looked at his evidence. The species that were able to live on when an environment rapidly changing were those who developed adaptable approaches and skill sets. The biggest and most cutthroat species were eventually phased out. That's why we don't have dinosaurs running up and down our streets today.

As we face new challenges to our time on the earth in the form of the climate crisis and perhaps other unknown pandemics, there are campaigns being run to forward status quo thinking while Darwin, African philosopher Credo Mutwa, and journalist Naomi Kline keep pointing to in their work—adaptation is the road to future success.

Technically speaking, adaptive learning is the process of custom learning experiences that address the unique needs of an individual through just-in-time feedback, pathways, and resources rather than providing a one-size-fits-all learning experience. Modern society has put a premium on the mechanized one-size-fits-all models at the expense of our ability to leverage great ideas from ordinary people best able to adapt. It's become trendy to eat street food, but innovation from the street and from the hood is more than culinary creativity. That ingenuity runs throughout our populations—from the well-to-do to the barely-making-it. Indeed, even today, we tend to mock the piece-together approaches of working-class communities because those adaptive ways aren't featured in Silicon Valley. Learning how to be adaptive requires whole life learning in real time to manage 'round-the-way and 'round-the-world change. This is the evolutionary bridge between two epochs. This is moving from one way of how life operates to another.

Adaptation means rethinking the very processes that got us to this point of crisis in the first place and replacing them with ones that are more in sync with the current time. It means considering new, innovative, and creative approaches to how we are to live going forward. It means embracing just the opposite of the ways that we've employed over the past few centuries. It means a complete re-evaluation of what works, what doesn't, and what can we do now with the tools at hand.

Both climate change and the COVID-19 pandemic are giving us clues as to how we are to deal with the coming challenges. However, many countries and individuals defaulted into old behavior (lack of transparency, deception, denial, and blame). From an evolutionary perspective, this presents a challenge to evolutionary theory: if this is a time of transition for society and the world, why don't these leaders exhibit *new* behaviors that would have the challenges more manageable? I would argue two points:

- The allure and benefits of power make it difficult for those in control to open the door for new ways forward.

- Evolutionary leadership and adaptive behavior people will emerge when old-world behavior starts to fail and cannot adapt to the demands of a new environment.

To that end, here are behaviors of leaders, organizers, and visionaries that are emerging now so that they may serve better over the next few years:

Adaptive leaders embrace opportunistic thinking. They literally see possibilities when others see the danger.

Adaptive people are resourceful. They have accumulated resources along the way and are now using their cache in their leadership role.

Adaptive people are looking down the road at what could happen. These people have a knack for looking ahead. And if they cannot see down the road, they call people who can.

Adaptive people see systems when other people see challenges. Systems are the infrastructure that keep a world operating in a certain way. Adaptive people understand that infrastructure, like everything else, needs to evolve, change, or reform to be successful in an evolving, changing, or reforming environment.

Adaptive people operate from a set of values. One of the great challenges of the old world is that a sense of values—guiding moral principles –are absent. People were and are making decisions based on situational ethics—that is, decisions that were based on ideas that met the personal needs of the decision-makers at that time. This conflicted with the image that a shared set of values existed between leaders and communities. Adaptive people have a tendency to restore the faith of fair play and trust as currency, recognizing the new world will rely on them.

Adaptive people keep their minds open when others are closed down. In times of crisis, status quo thinkers tend to play "small ball" at a time that asks them to go big. Why? Small ball, or reducing variables and risk, *seems* to make things more manageable in a time of stress. Adaptive people see just the opposite. They believe keeping their minds open for things they did not see before is the best way to manage the tumultuous time of change that we are in. New challenges will need new ideas as opposed to small, often used ideas. Adaptive people understand this.

Learning how to be adaptive in a time of transition is not a cliff note from a motivational speech. It is a highly developed survival technique that folk on the ground understand. It stands in stark contradiction to those who want to "conserve" ideas that simply don't work in a new environment. Adaptive learners are often called "early adapters" because of their ability to navigate a changing environment first. As Darwin so accurately suggested, this is not about the strongest, fastest, or smartest, but about those who are able to understand that we have to do something different.

6

If Black lives don't matter, none of our lives matter.
The basics of valuing human life and safety.

One of the most notorious crises in the United States is the ugly and never-ending confrontational relationship between the State (the police) and communities of color, particularly African Americans. Before we take another step into this centuries-old dance of violence, let's clarify a few points:

- While one can trace the practice of policing as far back historically as 27 BC in ancient Rome, the heart, soul, and meat-on-the-bones of modern policing in the United States was inspired by the slave patrols of the southern states.

- While more White people are killed by the police in the United States than other ethnic groups because of their sheer numbers, a much higher percentage of Black people are shot in high-profile and questionable extrajudicial killings.

- The practice of authorities or police killing unarmed Black people has a 400-year-old history in the US.

- The nation's extraordinarily high incarceration rate of Black men relative to the overall incarceration rate in the world reflects a punitive, industrial construct.

- The dramatic level of income inequality in 2020 demonstrates how systems have worked against Black wealth creation for centuries.

- Ongoing neighborhood segregation, under-funding of schools, underemployment, and general racial discrimination fuel a permanent underclass in the African American community that police departments are used to "keep in check."

In many ways, police violence against Black people captures the infrastructure that doesn't value Black lives and seeks to actively thwart efforts to create Black and Brown lives of quality and dignity.

I was recently invited to moderate an online panel discussion organized by Tilt West, a nonprofit dedicated to fostering conversation of art, humanity, and community. My fellow panelists included Wisdom Amouzou, an activist, diversity expert, and principal of Empower Community High School; Bianca Mikhan, a poet and an artist who focuses on mental and spiritual health in marginalized communities; and Lady Speech, a spiritual coach and advocate for LGBTQ communities. We were invited to reflect on Black safety in the face of ongoing police violence. I started our conversation by asking that we reimagine what safety might be. Is it solely about protecting ourselves from those who seek to kill us? Or does the notion of Black safety provoke a deeper question about finding true security in the quality of our lives? Is it both and more?

Mikhan argued for an idea of safety that reaches beyond our individual selves so that we may survive and thrive collectively. She believes that true safety is found in compassion. Mikhan's remarks raised hard questions about humanity. She reflected on the fact that some people have responded to the COVID-19 pandemic by buying guns, while others have baked bread. She said that we've been forced to ask the question of who we want to be as a society when we grow up, which provokes further questions such as whether we believe that people are fundamentally good. For Mikhan, it is our ability to apply our greatest selves to small domestic challenges that prepares us to create a bigger, better version of humanity.

Amouzou asserted that a truly safe environment requires three essential elements: freedom from threat, or not having to deal with the possibility of death on an ongoing basis; freedom from fear, or accepting that threat is part of the human experience; and peace, or living in a world where you can successfully manage threat and fear.

Lady Speech made the case that true safety is rooted in our relationship with Mother Earth. The broken relationship between humanity and the Earth creates the conditions which lead to state-sponsored violence. White supremacy and capitalism have disconnected us from Mother Earth and have resulted in a fear-based approach to life that shows up in all of our institutions. Lady Speech added that the 400 years of violence inflicted on African Americans have not been lost on Mother Earth, who is responding to the energy of this pain and trauma.

Our conversation also touched on what it feels like to walk around in a state of constant fear. Amouzou suggested that he manages this fear by mentally and emotionally departing from America. Mikhan responded that this kind of mental departure is essential to survival in American society. By contrast, Lady Speech believes that we must first come to terms with our traumatic history; we must acknowledge the effects that our violent history has on the present, by seeing the ways that the rapes of children and adults that were a common part of the African American slave experience impact our community even today.

My conversation with these three seers led me to create a list of seven ways that we might establish true safety and make it a way of life going forward.

1. *Bring back connection to the ancestors.* One of the most common indigenous African philosophical constructs is the idea of ancestral veneration. A basic scientific principle is that energy is never destroyed; it is simply transformed. This principle must also apply to human energy. Ancient people understood this as a basic truth of human experience and felt a profound, ongoing connection with their ancestors. This connection helped them face challenges

from a position of strength and with a perception of protection and safety.

2. *Embrace Ubuntu.* Ancestral veneration is rooted in the concept of Ubuntu. This idea says that "a person is a person because of other persons." In other words, none of us exists alone; we are not really individuals. We belong to a collective of people who have existed for millennia. This understanding stands in direct conflict with the Western notion of rugged individualism. True safety may be found by tapping into the genetic memory of that indigenous wisdom.

3. *Take the painting off the wall.* If you go back far enough (and sometimes not that far) almost every ethnic group has used song and dance, not for the purpose of artistic display, but as an integrated part of daily life. Somehow, in Western civilization, art has become something we collect and view at a distance, like a painting on the wall of a museum. Perhaps re-engaging with spontaneous music and dance would bring us closer to a way of life more in keeping with a safe environment. There is safety in the release provided by song and dance.

4. *Focus on quality of life.* One of my own anecdotal observations is that when people have a decent quality of life, they are less likely to accept an unsafe environment. They become committed to maintaining their safety, the safety of their family, and the safety of their community. When their lives are precarious, they will end up in unpredictable, perilous, and unsafe circumstances. The math here is not that hard.

5. *Defund the police?* Yes, I know this phrase is a lightning rod, but that's only because it has been highly politicized. Even more, something is amiss. According to a *New York Times* report from June 12, 2020, city police budgets across the country have risen by millions of dollars annually—even during lean years for city finances, and through a steep nationwide decline in violent crime that began in the early 1990s. More dollars are being funneled to police departments to fight a "ghost" out-of-control crime rate at the expense of

other city services. Police in the US have also become more militarized with assault-style weapons and even tanks from arms makers. The military industrial complex has come to see police departments as an expanding, secondary market that increases their profit margin. "Defunding the police" doesn't mean eliminating police from your city. It simply means better budgeting so that resources are not focused on putting more armed men and women on the streets with more weapons, inviting violent altercations. It means applying some of those funds instead to necessary services that address mental health, food scarcity, addiction, and other challenges that have been exacerbated by massive income inequality. Police budgets should not be tied to political whim, but to overall crime trends and statistics. Science, data, and truth should still matter.

6. *Support relationships.* The more we devote time and resources to developing and strengthening relationships among family and friends, the more we can tap into those relationships to help family members overcome challenges instead of leaving that responsibility to the police. Traditionally, families have been the first line of defense in a crisis. Without this support, we call on the police to step in where family could be the first call. This is not to say there aren't times when the police *should* be called, but imagine a society that supports families with the resources to provide more family-based services.

7. *Stop creating the "procariat."* If you combine the words precarious (unstable) with proletariat (working class), you create the word "procariat." Millions of Americans live the life of the "procariat"—the unstable working class—especially African Americans. If you cannot plan for the next eighteen months, you are living an unsafe life. If your household is food insecure, you are living an unsafe life. If you don't know where your next paycheck will come from, you are living an unsafe life. When we start to address these issues, we will improve safety for African Americans and halt the perpetuation of the procariat.

We have opportunities to do something about safety; they are not beyond us. They don't even require us to leave the comfort of our homes. They do, however, require a shared philosophy of Ubuntu that helps us understand that when others around us are unsafe, *we are all unsafe.*

7

Rugged individualism makes no sense
in this time of change.

The Corona Virus pandemic that devastated the US has been a story of bad management. You may not necessarily stop the emergence of novel virus, but good management can keep it from becoming a catastrophe. It's not because the US doesn't have the tools, resources, or personnel to manage it; it's because our political structure has peddled a thinly veiled "me" over "we" concept disguising itself as a personal choice or "rugged individualism." Other countries have made the pandemic manageable by making sure they put the good of the community first. Managing crises for the greater good of a community is the hallmark of civilized societies. Western individualism or what used to be colloquially called "rugged individualism" is the belief that everyone makes it on their own without the help of others. Of course, if you ask most millionaires (if you want to use money as a determinant of "making it"), they will tell you that their contacts, networks, generational wealth, government support programs, and racial advantage testify that they didn't make it on their own. They had an amazing amount of help and support. Yet, individualism, as it is popularly painted in US society, is a persistent ghost that now shows up as dysfunction, selfishness, and the breakdown of civility. But why would a society perpetuate an idea that works against its best interest? The reality is that it works for the best interest of a small number of wealthy people. These people want you to believe that you are on your own so that they can dis-empower cooperative organizations like unions which rely on the group over the individual. It allows them to keep you from being their next competition. Even the wealthy self-help authors and speakers are constantly telling you that if you just become better, you'll be rich and famous. The reality is that for hundreds of thousands and millions of years, humans have always relied on each other to create surviving and thriving success. Some self-help authors and rugged individualists are preaching a gospel that is against the understanding of our genetic memory. It's not a surprise that so many people are falling apart in a system that says it's all about you, while our DNA keeps saying it's all about all of us. Rugged individualism creates a cognitive dissonance that is spreading as anxiety, self-loathing, and depression.

The suicide epidemic in the "cowboy west."

An old mythos in the United States is one of the singular cowboys that basically solves his problems by himself, as an individual. This myth has been fueled over the years in Western cowboy movies, based primarily on romanticized versions of how early America functioned. This lone-wolf cowboy ups and settles the affairs of others and his own without the use of support groups or mental health resources. The message is that real men don't need other people to help them solve their problems. They just need to be tough and work it out. It is that false narrative that may be contributing to the dramatic rise of suicides in the high mountain West. Nationally, suicides have contributed to a four-year trend in the reduction of life expectancy in the US, with a definitive spike in Western states. Linda Goodman, the chief clinical officer at Peak Wellness Center in Cheyenne, said people suffering from depression or other issues in Wyoming and other rural states resist seeking assistance from counselors. In an interview in the April 2019 edition of Cowboy State Daily, Goodman says "The mentality that 'I just need to cowboy up and be tough.' That rugged individualism says, 'I need to be able to handle my problems by myself.'"

The exit from basic civility.

In his book *Bowling Alone*, author Robert Putnam discussed trends where Americans are divorcing themselves from civic organizations that build community ties, civility, and connectedness. He suggests that this is primarily due to technology that allows us to create personal silos online. That's not necessarily true. Technology is a toaster. You can use Zoom to strengthen the ties you have with friends and family around the world. But if you have a predisposition to individualism, you'll use it to build silos and create barriers to others. You're even more prone to be an extremist because you don't get the benefit of a fully vetted and nuanced conversation.

Individualism is not big enough for what we need.

From health care to systemic racism to education to climate crisis, we face gigantic challenges of a generation that require collective action. Individualism is simply too inefficient and too ineffective to handle the scale of current changes and disruptions. It's not robust enough for what we need right now.

The Ubuntu Alternative

There is a concept out of Africa called "Ubuntu." At its heart is the basic philosophy that we are all connected, and our strength is in leveraging that connectedness. This is the exact opposite of the rugged individual mythos and a more accurate reflection of how success is actually achieved. It is not an idea to get rid of individualism. *Rather, it is based on the understanding that individual parts work better together through interdependence.* At a time of monumental crises, it has the potential to be more agile and more flexible than what we've tried to date.

In an "every man for himself" world, we need a belief system that is more robust and innovative than what we've used so far. Let's open the door to something new.

8

Instead of talking about jobs, let's talk about opportunities.

It's just crazy that we're still talking about jobs like people did back more than one hundred years ago in the days of the Industrial Revolution. Over the years, we've heard economists, soothsayers, and observers speak of the coming loss of jobs due to the advancement of artificial intelligence and how robots would be the ones doing the theft. The essence of our conversation should be about "how do we create opportunity and abundance for a new way to live?" I'm not saying jobs are not a part of that mix. What I am saying is that we have to expand beyond the singular idea that jobs are the primary measurement of personal and community quality of life. That's obviously not true when you have people working two or three low-paying jobs and can barely make ends meet.

Before we talk about life beyond jobs, let me provide some clarity about the loss of jobs around the world, exacerbated by the COVID pandemic.

First of all, the robots aren't coming to take your jobs. They already have and are taking more and more of them every day.

In fact, they've been taking jobs all over the world since 1980 when global companies sought new ways of maximizing profits and shareholder value by reducing their biggest expense—employees. In the United States, the favorite complaint around job loss over the past 40 years has been that corporations are outsourcing to cheap labor in Mexico, India, and China. Yes, that's been a part of the mix, but the vast majority of jobs in the US have been lost to robotics and their efficiency. It's just more politically expedient to point to "cultural others" as the cause.

"The vast majority of lost US jobs—88 percent—were taken by robots and other homegrown factors that reduce factories' need for human labor."

— **Ball State University's Center for Business and Economic Research 2016**

To put a fine point on things, it's not that the robots have come to take your job. *They really are here to challenge the very concept of a job.* More and more companies are understanding that you simply don't need the same amount of labor to make the same amount of money. The expansion of advanced machines is a testament to efficiency. This, of course, cheapens jobs, which allows companies to keep wages fairly stagnant as they have for the past 40 years.

The COVID-19 pandemic has put the process of mechanizing industrial and mid-management jobs on steroids. A lot of the jobs that were lost during the crisis around the world simply aren't coming back. Why should they, now that companies have figured out how to operate without them during the pandemic?

It's important to put the job-loss dilemma in context. There is a belief that people around the world have always worked jobs. The assumption is that, since the days of the caveman, people have gotten up at the crack of dawn, punched a clock, and worked a 9–5. Some of this false reasoning has actually come from people who've watched the 1960s animated cartoon series *The Flintstones*. The idea of Fred Flintstone, a caveman, living hundreds of thousands of years ago, getting up in the morning and going through rush-hour traffic to get to Mr. Slate's quarry seemed like a reasonable facsimile of the truth for untold numbers. I hate to burst the bubble for some of you, but *The Flintstones* is a cartoon series, not a documentary. While we've always had work (laboring in our day-to-day life) the concept of job (laboring for someone else in mass) is only a little over a hundred years old. So the idea of job is a fairly new one in the history of humanity. This chapter on widespread and well-paying jobs for the masses is very much a story of the 20th century.

What will the new normal bring?

The new normal brings an opportunity for us to think through the concept of job, human value, and the contribution of humans to the community. But first, we need to understand more about the new world we've just entered.

There is a population bust happening in the world that's gaining speed.

Most, if not all, Western countries, as well as Russia, Japan, South Korea, and other parts of Europe and Asia, are no longer having enough children to replace the number of people dying. This is called a population bust. On the surface, this would seem like a good thing to those folks who believed our world was on the brink of disaster due to overpopulation. But that's not the case. Fewer and fewer people being born means fewer and fewer people able to work jobs, earn a living, buy a home, and provide a tax base for the community.

The world population is rapidly getting older.

The world is aging rapidly. There are fewer and fewer young workers in the world to support the society, particularly in the West. This group of the elderly also need more care and services than other demographics while this shortage of care workers will only get worse due to the COVID-19 pandemic.

Immigration reform around the world is in desperate need of an overhaul to meet the needs of a transforming world.

Nativist protests in countries around the world to keep out "the others" is like throwing gasoline on a raging fire of an older population with fewer young people and a diminishing tax base. Communities around the world need these younger workers but are dead set against having them. There is a deep need for immigration reform that matches the time we live in. Climate refugees due to extreme weather will further complicate these global challenges.

Our populations are getting dramatically older.

More jobs are going away due to robotics and artificial intelligence. Fewer people being born means fewer people of working age. Immigration reform is desperately needed so that working-age people can work in places that need them most. And let's not forget, we're at the beginning of a climate change crisis.

One answer to consider: The Regenerative Economy.

The new normal has provided the very foundation to re-imagine how economies work. If the past economies have generated income inequality, systemic racism, social disruption, natural world destruction, and exploitation and left the world on the brink of climate catastrophe, perhaps another kind of economy that does just the opposite is exactly what's needed. I would propose the Regenerative Economy. This construct would gear all social and economic activities of a community into restoring that which was lost while providing people with meaningful jobs of dignity. It is designed to galvanize our resources into regenerative efforts to mitigate the effects of climate change, create employment for those willing and able to work, create a reliable tax base, and put teeth behind efforts to end systemic racism and gender bias. We're talking about a community that can be consciously transformed to work for the greater good through free enterprise, economic strength, a values-based belief system while meeting the current needs of people today. This is not another take on sustainability, that is, keeping the current socioeconomic direction but finding ways of making it sustainable. This is organizing the purpose of an entire *community* to do good and do well. Here are some of the jobs that can and are being created through a Regenerative Economy effort.

Transforming empty lots.

This may be particular to the US, but there are other similar programs all around the world. The Environmental Protection Agency in the US defines a brownfield as a property, once used for commercial or industrial purposes, to be used and redeveloped in a sustainable way. There are over

450,000 such properties around the country, in every community. What would happen if we created jobs and enterprises around community gardens for food security, a renewable energy field, an electric automobile charging station, or an enterprise development center for communities of color? These are not new ideas; we're just organizing them around an entire community.

Construction work to rehabilitate buildings.

There is enough work for years in rehabilitating buildings and homes to become more energy efficient and act as a grid for distributive energy.

Paid activism.

One of the great challenges communities face is that not enough of their people understand that we live in a new normal and that we can revisit ideas that seemed extreme, weird, or exceptional. Paying activists to help people understand the level of change that's happening can make all the difference in developing a progressive tax base to fund this effort. The activists can use their skills in social media or through in-person events.

Disaster preparedness training.

As we've discussed previously in this book, there are other challenges waiting for us in the new normal. Our ability to manage these disasters will determine how we travel through this time. This is a job that doesn't require massive tech skills; thus, they would be more accessible to older or under-skilled people who find themselves out of a job because of the COVID-19 pandemic.

Techs to modernize our electric grid.

The updating of our national and global power grids to reflect a new world needs to happen immediately. Technicians who've worked in the field have an opportunity to expand their capacity while making room for more technicians to join them. It's a big job that takes a lot of time but will put people to work.

Creating recreational space and green space management.

An aspect of the new normal is that it offers us an opportunity to recapture things that were lost. One of those things lost being our connection to the land. By putting money behind the effort to create more recreational space, we create opportunities for people to find space during their day for mindfulness activities. It is one thing to talk about mindfulness, but it is another thing to create spaces that support the activities. Again, this isn't a high-tech job, so it leaves out fewer and fewer potential workers.

Developing regenerative entrepreneurs among disenfranchised communities.

Just as WeWork developed spaces for entrepreneurs of many different products, we can create a workspace where communities of color and the disenfranchised can have a chance to champion products, services, and tools that can reimagine how the world works.

Regenerative agriculture consultants.

Indigenous land caretakers who've learned ancient techniques from their ancestors. Agriculturalists who understand data application in modern farming. Back yard gardeners who picked up a few skills along the way. Employing them as teams to help develop food security around the world can change the game.

Tree planting.

The data still shows planting trees is a formidable beachhead to slow down the ravages of climate change. No skill level is needed for this opportunity.

Climate change weatherization.

The ability of homes to withstand the extreme weather conditions brought on by climate change will be crucial in saving lives, especially as our populations continue to get older. This is a prime area for job development.

Universal Basic Income.

Providing our populations with a basic income is the mark of an advanced and enlightened society. Think of what could happen if we leveraged the human potential of billions of ideas, creativity, and innovation instead of tying it up in a 9–5 grind.

Re-evaluating the job terrain of a new society means that we have to understand all of the factors that are reshaping the concept of job in our communities. We must also consider other economic structures that can produce jobs and work on behalf of our future at the same time. This is not an impossible task. It merely takes visionary leadership, a higher spirit, and courage.

9

Why a fear-based society will fail us every time.
Why an empathy-based one will always win the day.

Fear may be the most powerful motivator in the world. Some people have learned to utilize fear to motivate people to do their bidding. The problem with fear besides the obvious exploitation of people is how ongoing fear manipulation in a society has a way of diminishing the population's quality of life. A University of Minnesota report from their May 2016 newsletter indicated that ongoing fear does the following:

Deterioration of physical health. Fear weakens our immune system and can cause cardiovascular damage, gastrointestinal problems such as ulcers and irritable bowel syndrome, and decreased fertility. It can lead to accelerated aging and even premature death.

Memory loss. Fear can impair the formation of long-term memories and cause damage to certain parts of the brain, such as the hippocampus. This can make it even more difficult to regulate fear and can leave a person anxious most of the time. To someone in chronic fear, the world looks scary and their memories confirm that.*Brain processing and reactivity.* Fear can interrupt processes in our brains that allow us to regulate emotions, read nonverbal cues and other information presented to us, reflect before acting, and act ethically. This impacts our thinking and decision-making in negative ways, leaving us susceptible to intense emotions and impulsive reactions. All of these effects can leave us unable to act appropriately.

Mental health. Other consequences of long-term fear include fatigue, clinical depression, and Post-Traumatic Stress Disorder.

A fear-based society has a striking ability to make its population sicker, more depressed, and dumber. Unfortunately, there are people who lean into fear as a means of power and control. Some of the other repercussions of a fear-based society include:

A fear-based society uses scarcity as a basis for markets. Some have, others don't, so the best way to earn a living is to control the markets to limit the availability of products. Those who control the means of production and distribution make a lot of money by charging a premium for the product based through artificial scarcity.

A fear-based society seeks to create the "cultural other." It is easy to rally a community if you can find, point to, develop, and demonize a cultural other—people who don't look or seem like you. Politicians and others seeking power are able to leverage this human survival tool by distorting the truth of the cultural other and make them appear more frightening and threatening than they actually are. History is filled with men who have been most successful in this process. Hitler, Stalin, Belgium King Leopold of the Congo, etc. Their fear-based foundation worked because it touched a defense mechanism that became a part of our humanity in the process of evolution. Fear is not a negative tool in and of itself. It's designed to keep us alive under duress. It does, however, become dangerous when unscrupulous people exploit it and their people for political and personal gain at the expense of others.

A fear-based society utilizes fear-based imagery to achieve goals. The logic goes that if God uses fear to achieve his goals, then why shouldn't I? Reminding those that are being manipulated of popular imagery that sell the story of an angry, jealous, and bitter God can be a powerful persuader for people to act out on these impulses.

So what would be the pillars of an empathy-based, affirmative, courageous, and visionary cultural society? There is evidence that a fear-based environment works directly against our wiring.

- A study in a May 6, 2020, edition of the *New York Times* called "The Science of Helping Out" suggested that we are at our best when we do for others, even "cultural others." An organizational psychologist by the name of Dr. Adam Grant performed a study on personal attitudes and psychological health during times of crisis and discovered that people who cope the best with crisis are those who help others. "When you talk other people through their problems, you come up with ways to manage your own," said Grant.

- Another 2018 study suggests that people who earn more money may be less likely to share their wealth than those who earn less. This study comes from the Queen Mary University of London and published in the journal *Basic and Applied Social Psychology*. The study suggests that people of lower economic status seek to participate in a cooperative economic model of sharing, while those who make more by chance or inheritance develop a belief that they should keep more of what they have.

- On February 13th, 2019, Dr. Waguih William IsHak wrote a stunning article in the blog of Cedar-Sinai hospital. The article was called *The Science of Kindness*. In the article, Dr. IsHak said that modern research suggests that acts of kindness can release hormones that contribute to your mood and overall well-being. The practice is so effective it's being formally incorporated into some types of psychotherapy. The research suggests that it's a chemical reaction. Why kindness makes us feel better has centered around oxytocin. Sometimes called "the love hormone," oxytocin plays a role in forming social bonds and trusting other people. It's the hormone mothers produce when they breastfeed, cementing their bond with their babies. Oxytocin is also released when we're physically intimate. It's tied to making us more trusting, more generous, and friendlier, while also lowering our blood pressure.

- In an article published in *Psychology* magazine on January 1, 2015, it is suggested that evolution is the culprit behind our potential kind nature. The article, entitled "We Are Wired to

Be Kind: How Evolution Gave us Empathy, Compassion and Gratitude," suggests the strengthening of our capacity for sympathy and empathy played a central role in human development.

These studies line up with the ancient philosophical concept of Ubuntu: "A person is a person because of other people." This is in direct conflict with a fear-based, "others"-based reign of the day. The suggestion here also leans into another idea. What are the adverse effects of a society that is fear based when our deepest wiring suggests that a loving, connected idea of ourselves is in our intuitive and chemical nature? Are we creating a massive cognitive dissonance that may be creative collective mental and spiritual health crises? And what about a society that leans into our strengths of altruism? Would it be possible we'd create greater, stronger, visionary communities?

When we live in a fear-based society, we simply aren't living our best life. In fact, it can be argued that it is our worst life. Its only remedy is to be replaced by an overriding theme of courage, vision, sharing, and yes, love. It's science.

10

We need a new set of priorities for education and for leadership. Here are the crucial seven.

There are teachers across the planet, right now, tearing their remaining hair out because they are in a teaching morass. It is possible we may lose an entire generation of students in this transformational moment because the regular playbook has been thrown out of the window due to COVID. How do you teach online during a pandemic? What should be our priorities right now? What exceptions should we make for students during this time? What does the "new normal" for education look like? All of this is maddening. You don't know what being turned inside out is until you know what teachers are going through.

Even more, leaders in many countries think they have an idea of what leadership will look like in this new world. The problem is that many of those leaders are still drawing from Western models championed by Stephen Covey, Simon Sinek, or Peter Drucker. They are men for their time and culture. This world requires an entirely new kind of leadership and leadership model that incorporates the visions, ideas, and innovation of everyone, not just those who've had a cooler marketing campaign.

There are seven priorities that must take center stage to create people to manage this level of massive change.

1. We should teach Basic Connect Theory.

Basic Connect Theory or BCT is teaching from the perspective that connectedness is a constant in the universe as well as in the natural world that surrounds us, thus, providing a blueprint for success for future systems and socioeconomic structures. From how the cycle of life works to how our technology points to efficiency in connectedness, BTC is the foundation of how students can build a reimagined future. Make no mistake, a more connected world is more efficient but it also makes all of us vulnerable to the same threats, as demonstrated in the COVID-19 crisis. The flip side is that with all of us in the challenge together, we can gather more resources, human power, and innovation in handling those same crises instead of leaving ourselves exposed to the whims of a few countries that might or might not decide to sign on and help. The climate change crisis is a perfect example of what happens in a world where individual needs overwrites the needs of everybody else. At the writing of this book, we have yet to meet the goals set to address the Paris Climate Accord CO_2 emissions rules to slow down the rate of the climate crisis. This is mostly because some nation-states refuse to participate, believing that saving the planet from a long slow death works against their individual and immediate best interest. This logic is based on the idea that somehow you can be safe in one corner of your house, even though the rest of the house is on fire. Some would say this is simply humans being humans—self-interested, vain, self-indulgent. I would submit that this behavior has something to do with how our nation-states organize leadership systems. Teaching our future leaders to understand and implement BTC gives us a fighting chance to create better, efficient leadership models in a different environment.

2. We should help students pursue their curiosity.

Young minds are naturally curious. Why don't we formalize and champion this natural place as opposed to emphasizing old and staid basic requirements that reflect a 20th-century world? Many systems are designed to promote self-preservation, when they should be designed to promote the power of curiosity. Curiosity is the tool that allows us to go beyond the known and ask questions of the unknown. Having the courage to drill down on essential questions frees us from the stifling effect of what happens when we get stuck on "what's in it for me?" We ignore the power of curiosity at our own peril. The COVID-19 pandemic has exposed that blind spot in our thinking. Curiosity development in students isn't a nice dessert to have alongside a main course of common core. It *is* the main course in the new world emerging.

There are three major benefits that fostering curiosity develops in students and leadership which allow effective transformation and transition to occur more smoothly in a challenged and changing world.

One of the most powerful benefits that curiosity brings is the ability to foster an openness to new experiences and new ideas. One of the big challenges many countries faced during the early part of the COVID-19 pandemic was that there was an inability to look beyond systems they already had in place to battle something that was above and beyond what they had experienced before. Curiosity about this new challenge could have opened them up to transparency, innovation, and new ways of dealing with problems. In a *Forbes* magazine article in March of 2017, called "What Happens When Leaders Lack Curiosity," testing showed that the single best thing that companies can do to promote diversity and inclusion is to hire leaders with high openness scores. They will not just be more willing to understand and connect with people who are different—both demographically and psychologically—but also create more diverse teams and inclusive cultures. On the other side of that coin, when leaders lack curiosity, they will hire in their own image, creating homogeneous teams where differences are stigmatized rather than celebrated. That homogeneity is not just regulated to their hires. It also creates status quo thinking. This can be the worst possible kind of thinking in a time of dramatic change and challenge.

Another benefit of curiosity development is that a curious mindset has a higher tolerance for the unknown. If you wanted to find out what scares most people, it is the myth of the unknown. We say myth because most people don't understand how the unknown works. Tomorrow is the unknown, yet we live as if the day is promised. Most of our existence is navigating the unknown. The myth is that some single event in the future is unknown and everything else is assured.

The curious mind navigates this space, not with a disregard for most people's tolerance of the unknown, but with a healthy respect for the unknown as a way of life. Curiosity somehow allows people who possess it to build a bridge over the waters of the unknown, understanding that there is an ongoing chance they might fall in those choppy waters. They simply build the bridge anyway. Even more, the curious mind does a mix of three major streams—data, experience, and intuition. These are the same streams myself and other futurists lend to come up with a reasonable view of the road ahead. Curious minds mix these streams and have a broader capacity for answers than non-curious minds.

The curious mind also is more likely to accept their mistakes and missteps in their decision-making. The non-curious have an urge for closure on their mistakes so that no one knows that they were responsible. This kind of closure is a form of self-defense. Again, these are the kind of actions we saw entire countries take at the beginning of the COVID-19 pandemic before having to reconcile their self-defense with the obvious growing cases of the virus in their states.

Another indicator of a curious mind (but certainly not restricted to it) is that curious minds often have a broader category of friends than a non-curious mind. As mentioned earlier, about high openness scores, curious minds extend their beliefs beyond business and professional worlds and into their personal worlds. They have managed to create friendships across racial, cultural, gender, and geographic lines because their curious mind won't let them get boxed in. Their friends, as well as their mental tool kit, are broader and bigger.

This sounds great for *identifying* a community and a curious leadership team, but how, if possible, can you develop curiosity?

There are seven things you can do with your team or community to bring out this highly desirable talent and trait.

Get students out of their comfort zone. Yeah, I know. We hear this all the time, but it cannot be emphasized enough. Global connections, more profound personal contacts, and shared experiences from different communities can give young people a bigger, broader capacity to think through challenges.

Create an environment of asking questions. We're not used to that. We think questioning means the person asking the question is weak because they don't already know. On the contrary, creating an environment that fosters questioning is a sign of how strong the education system is.

I don't want to paint a picture of the curious mind being above reproach. Curious students are subject to the same mistakes of false assumptions, cultural bias, and misinformation as the rest of us. They simply don't let those handicaps stand in their way to make courageous decisions.. The challenges of the world ahead include technological evolution, geopolitical realignment, climate change crisis, moving from a petroleum-based present to a renewable energy future, and socioeconomic transition that will be unlike anything we've seen before. Curious minds are the ones strong enough to navigate this level of change.

3. We must champion visionary thinking.

Vision, the ability to imagine and see possibilities beyond physical evidence, is usually left to politicians, leaders of faith, and CEOs as a tool of the ambitious and well connected. The truth is, young people have been born with it as part of the human package. Leaders have it as part of their intuitive selves. To what degree we develop it usually determines the quality of our lives. Even more, our degree of developing it will determine our readiness in managing the new challenges of the future. Here are three things you must do in developing your visionary leadership style.

Normalize vision as a part of the thought process. Imagine young people being bold enough to start predicting what's going to happen to our society and the world over the next few years, checking with other student groups about their testing results and checking with others about their plans to do something about the coming challenges. This shouldn't be an honors class special venture. This should be standard classroom 101. Think about it from this angle: Let us say you were in a conversation with your fiancé and asked them about their future plans, what do they see for your family, and how do they see themselves in the world. If they answered "I have no idea. I have not given it thought," you can be sure that you will develop a high degree of anxiety around trust in the relationship. You are marrying someone who does not seem to have a clue about things that will directly affect your quality of life. This is the same for our young people. If they are not thinking from a visionary place, how can we trust them with the future years? If you seek to navigate the new world emerging, you must provide your next set of leaders with the skills to do an honest assessment about the risks and opportunities ahead

Quit sending motivational speakers to "pump up" our people. Visionary thinking is NOT about painting a rose-colored view of the way forward. Unfortunately, those seeking to organize their communities and organizations for the changes to come to think this is how visionary leadership is done, so they send in motivational speakers—people with a non-nuanced view of the road ahead. That is a disservice to your people. There will be hard decisions and losses in this transition. Our job is not to sugarcoat the future but to give students and leaders the tools as a challenge to do something about the road ahead. Placating your people with "you can do anything" speeches is an easy way to create a lack of trust. Young people will soon discover that they *can't* do anything. What is true, is that they can try to do a lot of things, as they should. I wanted to play center for the Los Angeles Lakers Basketball Team, so you can imagine my disappointment in my high school basketball coach who told me I could do anything. I'm 6 feet. The average center in the NBA is 6 foot, 10 inches. As it is currently designed, I would not be successful as a center for the Lakers, so that is something I cannot do. Fortunately, I had other people around me who provided me with an honest assessment of my skill set and made some great suggestions. Let's give young people the hard facts and honesty they need to be successful in a new kind of world emerging.

Consult your brain trust. Visionary thinking is not developed in a vacuum. It is the process of gathering data so that you can come to a solid, clear, and qualified guess at the road ahead. The best path to success in a time of rapidly changing scenarios is to get a wider range of ideas and thoughts on a subject. Consult family members. Develop a relationship with a mentor. Consult your friendly neighborhood futurist (ah-um). Check in with colleagues around the world,

Use vision as a powerful unifier. I would submit that when an organization, a country, city, or community is in discord, the lack of a common vision is usually at the center of the problem. Vision doesn't mean everyone agrees on an item. It means that the vision or a view of the road ahead is so big, inclusive, affirmative, and compelling, people are willing to put aside their differences to make that one thing happen, first and foremost. If people are not embracing your vision, it may not be big enough. Help young people understand that from vision, laws, infrastructure, and policy emerge.

Vision makes you put in work. Most people may not look at vision as a process, but it is. It requires you to flesh out a passing thought or idea. It demands that you think it through so that It's more than a vision or a dream. It's an action plan. Vision requires you to make, at least, a mental commitment to something that used to be fringe or a blip on your radar. Developing the vision means you are now committed to seeing something through.

Vision is not a silver bullet to solving our problems, but it is a powerful tool, especially in a world during the transition. Anyone talking about the status quo in a time of change should raise a red flag in your mind. A time of transition is asking us to expand our capacity of what is possible. This is where true leadership starts to emerge—through vision.

Feminine Principle Leadership must become first nature to us. **Feminine Principle Leadership** is an all-encompassing idea that leadership is best when empathetic, considerate, lateral, and based on shared responsibility and shared benefits. While it is being called Feminine Principle Leadership, the foundation is based on the ideas of Ubuntu. The reason this leadership model is called Feminine Principle Leadership is that it reflects the feminine tendencies in human interaction, particularly in the ways that mothers engage children and other family members. The most important questions of this leadership model are "Is everyone okay?" "Is everyone being fed?" "Are you being kind?" "How can I help?" "Are you sharing your things?" "Are you looking out for one another." To be clear, feminine principle leadership is not the exclusive domain of women. It is a human idea.

How can the application of Feminine Principle Leadership better manage the coming challenges of unknown crises? How does this management model compare to contemporary best practices?

The real strength of Feminine Principle Leadership is the capacity it can provide to management. During the early part of the COVID-19 pandemic, the Government of Denmark told private companies struggling with drastic measures to curb the spread of the COVID-19 virus, that they would cover 75 percent of employee salaries if they promised not to cut staff. This bold move did the following:

- Relatively speaking, it stabilized the business community as it navigates the unknowns of a pandemic.

- It provides clarity for workers and helps reduce anxiety.

- It provides a definitive plan while the government works on other parts of the challenge.

This reflection of Feminine Principle Leadership asks the basic question, "Is everyone alright?" This is not a warm and fuzzy platitude, but a concrete form of response based on a philosophical construct. The definitive nature of this response puts the government leadership in a place to make clear decisions based on caring for the greater good of the body they govern as well as provide confidence and goodwill among the people it serves. It should also be noted that Denmark has one of the highest tax rates in the world, so it is reasonable to expect a robust government response to serving its people in a crisis. But the essence of governments is to provide support and protection for their citizens. If it is not doing this basic function, *what is it doing?*

Would the challenges of history be different if Feminine Principle Leadership were applied to past leadership crisis moments? Let us pose these questions in "what if" scenarios.

- In the March 2015 edition of *Scientific American*, a report was released that indicated Exxon knew, in 1981, about climate change and the challenges it would pose to the world. They chose, instead, to embark on a mission of disinformation to protect their profits potentials. In theory, if Feminine Principle Leadership was the leadership model of Exxon at that time, it is possible a different set of questions would have been asked, perhaps leading to a different 45-year decision. Questions would have revolved around how do we make sure everyone is okay, or how do we look out for one another under these circumstances, or even how can we help create a new set of options from this?

- Would the French Revolution have happened at all if Marie Antoinette and her husband operated from Feminine Principle Leadership and asked questions like "Is everyone being fed?" or "Are you being kind?" or "Are the children alright?"

- Would the Herero and Nama massacre of 1904–1908 have happened if the German colonizers had asked not how to take land from the indigenous populations of then Southwest Africa, now Namibia, but instead asked if they could create ways to share the land, their wealth, and friendship. It is worth asking if a different leadership model would have saved the lives of nearly 100,000 people from being gassed to death in the first case of genocide and ethnic cleansing in the 20th century.

Feminine Principle Leadership is the direct opposite of the command and control leadership model that emphasizes control in the hands of the few. In some ways, the challenges of the day are a referendum on the command and control leadership model. Is it sustainable? Can it be transformed to become something better? Does it have a flexible capacity under duress? Is the bureaucracy created under it nimble enough to manage an immediate crisis? What has been the command and control track record? Should we engage in another model that is more in keeping with the challenges we now face? The challenge of change and transition means that models that have little room for flexibility and efficiency will become more and more problematic.

We must learn how to anticipate future "Black Swans." When the COVID-19 virus swept into the world, many societies were overwhelmed simply because they had not anticipated something as comprehensive as this pandemic. But if one were to read enough of the material surrounding pandemics, one could have easily predicted the crisis and, in some cases, even avoided the full brute force of it.

Black swan events are unexpected, or not predicted that happen out of the blue and go on to shake the very foundation of an organization or society. While many organizations have emergency preparedness plans on the books, black swan events have a clever way of catching us off guard. Even more, by their very nature, they are things that we cannot prepare for. In other words, the plans on the books are only guidelines and suggestions based on the *last* black swan event as a model.

While there is a narration making the rounds that the COVID-19 pandemic was completely unexpected, the evidence says otherwise. Apparently, it had been anticipated by experts for some time. Further evidence shows that it was not only predicted but anticipated by governments around the world, especially those who had the unfortunate experience of dealing with the SARS pandemic as well as the H1N1 pandemic. With this in mind, how could so many in the world be so dramatically unprepared for something like this? The unpreparedness was complicated by an initial lack of transparency in reporting and trying to utilize a 20th-century skill set in a world that demands 21st-century approaches.

In order to navigate the world of the immediate future, we must now develop teams whose entire job is to anticipate the future and help mitigate "black swans." Allowing this level of thinking to be part of your process does not take away the risk, but helps it to become more manageable. No, you do not need a team of thousands or a giant budget to manage this level of risk. In ancient kingdoms, a chief executive needed a "seer" or someone whose top job was to look ahead and anticipate things to come.

We must address income inequality as part of change and transitional management. Here are three reasons why change and transitional management cannot or should not be separated from the problem of income inequality. This must be taught in schools and in leadership workshops.

1. The COVID-19 pandemic has exposed how vulnerable working-class families and the poor are, due to years of a widening global income inequality gulf. At this writing, it appears that those who have the least resources are the ones most negatively affected by the current pandemic. Higher death rates, more people out of work, and no resources to care for loved ones are only a few of the challenges that plague working-class families as the gulf between the rich and the poor continues to widen.

2. Income inequality has already made it difficult for the working poor to manage day-to-day living, even before the mass change occurs. According to a 2018 report from the United States, called "The Fourth National Climate Assessment," income inequality keeps vital resources away from communities that need them most in dealing with day-to-day challenges. Working poor communities are in no position to deal with the jolt of massive, systemic change unless we re-prioritize spending and access to resources.

3. Let's make sure we share all available information with the people who are most directly affected by the upcoming crises of scale. Giving people a fighting chance to defend themselves in the face of change that will turn their worlds upside down is the first order of business for modern leadership. The second order is to build out solutions that support everyone.

We must make racial equity and empowerment our mission-critical priority. For too long we've allowed a global system to maintain racial and gender inequality established eons ago in the old paradigm. We claim that we are not participating in those wrongs, yet we regularly embrace the benefits we're provided from that same infrastructure on automatic pilot. The indigenous wisdom, ideas from a new perspective, collective support, and bold leadership were all lost in the prior world due to systemic racism and bias. The new normal recognizes that the best use of all resources is to bring everyone in. There is an untold amount of social capital we left on the table because we wanted to show that we were "better" than "them." That thought is not only embarrassingly simple minded, but it has proved deadly to those left behind. Leaving some out due to personal preference is a vanity we cannot afford in the face of an extinction-level event like climate crisis. Platitudes and fundraising dinners to give us pats on the back for our good work haven't worked. Establishing a new foundation will.

Many of these ideas have been shared before. However, these are the things we should drill down with students and leaders if we want to create leadership that is ready and appropriate for this moment.

11

Ubuntu – the right belief at the right time.

Belief is basically defined as trust or faith in someone or something. Belief is the driver that determines everything we say or do. When we talk about belief in the context of the new normal, we're not necessarily talking about religion, but rather the shared set of ideas or values that a community with diverse religions embraces in order to operate. This shared set of beliefs can work with different faith traditions and can work across cultural platforms, geographic locations, and ideas. An example of a shared belief would be a phrase found in almost every faith tradition: "Do unto others as you would have them do unto you." While "do unto others" is a well-known and shared idea, it is not the lens through which current leadership has operated. A more accurate philosophical belief that defined how the pre-COVID world worked is: some get, most don't.

It may not be a formal belief, but the de facto results are proof positive this is an underlying driver. From this belief, our policies, laws, infrastructure, and resources are allocated. Our belief is the lens that guides our decision-making. The new normal provides an opportunity for us to re-examine that core belief and an opportunity to implement a new kind of belief that would be more in keeping with a re-imagined time of transformation. This philosophical construct of "some get, most don't" has a negative embedded in its premise. It is assuming a binary idea that simply isn't big enough for the moment. It's not that resources aren't finite and there aren't limits on how things are managed. But the decisions that we make from this single belief has created our worst challenges:

- Climate crisis is the result of a belief that some can use the resources of the planet at the expense of many, even as that use threatens all life on earth.

- Income inequality is the result of concentrating wealth in the hands of a few while taking away resources from the many.

- Systemic racism is the result of the belief that some people are more deserving than others and we can implement practices that reflect that myth.

- Food insecurity assumes that even though our current world distribution system wastes almost half of all food produced, we don't have enough to rid the world of hunger.

- Political corruption makes peace with the idea that malfeasance, grift, and theft are justified if they result in personal gain.

- Poverty is the direct manifestation of the idea that there is not enough to go around even though 10 percent of the population has more wealth and resources than the remaining 90 percent.

Most organizations that seek to make a better world have concentrated their energies on the symptoms or results of the belief system as opposed to dealing with the core issue from which all of our actions flow—our belief or our values. Everything starts with belief.

Ubuntu is big enough for this moment.

The new normal provides an opportunity to explore and implement the characteristics of a new shared belief: We are all connected.

While this is a version of the "do unto others as you would have them do unto you" concept, a new version of this idea is necessary. The African concept of Ubuntu provides the agility communities need in order to be more flexible in an environment of constant and ongoing change and challenges. Some of the benefits of an Ubuntu belief system could include the following:

- If we believe all people and all things are connected, we'll be able to creatively redesign infrastructure that sees the environment as an extension of ourselves. A policy that reflects this belief would mean new priorities around climate crisis and perhaps a more aggressive approach to climate change mitigation and adaptation.

- If we believe all people and all things are connected, more robust economic systems will be developed that will account for prevailing poverty. The focus will be on making sure our systems execute shared abundance which would reduce poverty, if not eliminate it altogether.

- Systemic racism would be seen as a direct conflict to our core belief and help us to develop a policy that would address this challenge as a priority. Everything from police shootings, the prison industrial complex, global exploitation, and human trafficking would get the resources needed to end their practices simply because our money follows our policies.

- Political corruption would be greatly reduced because our belief would be that theft, malfeasance, and deception are morally repugnant and worthy of the highest application of the law. Once our laws reflect our new beliefs, the laws will have the teeth to reinforce what we collectively share as values.

- Restorative justice (the idea of creating criminal punishment that helps restore the community from the wrongdoing rather than exact revenge) would be seen as a way forward into a new criminal justice system.

- Food waste would be outlawed and force us to create new systems that reflect this.

Changing our core belief doesn't mean we'll experience instant success into a new normal. It only means re-evaluating a belief to see if it works for the future, for the time we find ourselves in, and for the greater good. Fortunately, the new normal has provided us with a window to do due diligence on something we may not have questioned before. If that core belief is working against our quality of life and threatening our very existence, doing a re-examination is simply prudent and wise.

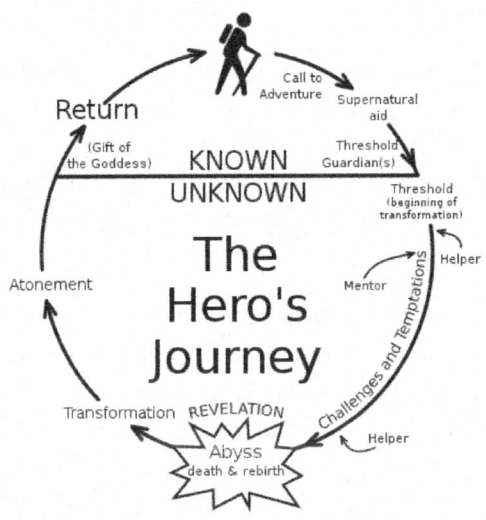

Conclusion

We are in the dark night of the soul. And that's a good thing....

In the many years I spent as a support coach for homeless residents at the Samaritan House homeless shelter here in Denver, Colorado, I always used The Hero's Journey as a tool to help my clients understand what was happening to them. For those of you who don't know, The Hero's Journey is an ancient construct of storytelling, often used by The Yoruba of West Africa, in ancient Greek mythology and Native and Central American diety stories. In this construct, all of us take off in an area of known facts and experiences. As we continue the journey, we end up in the unknown, run into a major conflict, then end up in a crisis....a dark night of the soul that potentially is totally destructive. In the middle of crisis, we either become destroyed under the weight of the moment or rise to become transformed and greater than ever before as we return on a new journey.

Welcome to the dark night of the soul.

We are there. Right now. Here in the States and around many parts of the world.

The series of recent, current and future pandemics, centuries old systemic racism, unprincipled and unethical political operatives, expanding income inequality, firmly entrenched misogyny, ignored climate crisis, legalized bribery, and the philosophy of "every man for himself" have brought us to this moment in time where we have to decide who we want to be when we grow up.

Some would approach the dark night of the soul with dread because of how it takes us deeply into the unknown and often, with pain. But we must remember, pain is not the same as suffering. Pain comes when transition happens, such as the birth of a child. Suffering is when we choose to make the pain a negative and ugly affair. As you leave the room you are in, you pass through the door into a new room and new opportunities. The direct next room we step into is to transformation, but only if we choose it. We could stay in our current room and be locked in darkness.

We are all now standing at that door with a decision to make. We are being asked to either embrace our darker, uglier human elements of selfishness, violence, racism, stupidity and arrogance or step into our transformation with power and strength. Choosing the latter puts us on a new path, a new journey of greatness we would never have chosen had it not been for the dark night of the soul. Let's face it....most of us would never embrace new ideas, a new path and a new vision unless we were forced into the moment. We're here. That's why the Dark Night Of The Soul can be a blessing if we see it as such.

As a futurist, I see us making a wise choice in this moment. I also see a new era being ushered in, not by the work of the politicians, but by the voters who recognized how close we came to the edge of the abyss because we were sleeping on the job. Even more, the challenges we face require all shoulders at the wheel. This moment cannot be left up to old men in suits to decide for us. As the evidence demonstrates, they are out of their depth for this new phase. This prediction that we will choose well does take into account the illegal and unethical shenanigans of unsavory humans who will not respect our decision. My prediction is simply that we will choose correctly and will defend our decision and the new, transformed path we will now walk on.

My sincere hope is that this short book will provide you with some new ideas and a vision into the new journey we are to embark upon. And let us remember the ancient African proverb...

> *"If your vision is for a year plant wheat, if you vision is for a decade plant trees, and if your vision is for a lifetime plant people."*

Let's now plant for a new life and world by giving tender care to a new crop of people and the ideas embedded in their hearts.

Keep the faith, baby.